Contents

A Message to Peers . . . .

Where Is God? ***Topic: God*** (Side One) . . . . 5 & 7

Why Are There So Many Religions? ***Topic: Church*** (Side Two) . . . . 6 & 8

Why Are Parents So Annoying? ***Topic: Parents or Guardians*** (Side One) . . . . 9 & 11

Why Do I Fight So Much with My Siblings? ***Topic: Family*** (Side Two) . . . . 10 & 12

How Can I Learn to Control My Temper? ***Topic: Anger and Hate*** (Side One) . . . . 13 & 15

Why Do People Fight over Silly Things? ***Topic: Conflict*** (Side Two) . . . . 14 & 16

Does God Have a Specific Purpose for Me? ***Topic: The Future*** (Side One) . . . . 17 & 19

Why Is School So Boring? ***Topic: School*** (Side Two) . . . . 18 & 20

Why Are There So Many Temptations in Life? ***Topic: Morals*** (Side One) . . . . 21 & 23

What Makes a Good Decision? ***Topic: Choices*** (Side Two) . . . . 22 & 24

Why Are Young People Using Drugs and Alcohol?
Topic: Drugs and Alcohol (Side One) . . . . 25 & 27

Is Smoking Going to Kill Me? ***Topic: Smoking*** (Side Two) . . . . 26 & 28

Who Decides What Popular Is? ***Topic: Image*** (Side One) . . . . 29 & 31

Why Is Life So Difficult? ***Topic: Stress*** (Side Two) . . . . 30 & 32

What Is a True Friend? ***Topic: Friends*** (Side One) . . . . 33 & 35

Why Do People Care If They Are Popular? ***Topic: Peer Pressure*** (Side Two) . . . . 34 & 36

Why Did My Friend Die? ***Topic: Death*** (Side One) . . . . 37 & 39

Why Do We Feel a Need to Cover Up Our Feelings? ***Topic: Emotions*** (Side Two) . . . . 38 & 40

Why Don't Guys Think Like Girls? ***Topic: Girls and Guys*** (Side One) . . . . 41 & 43

If We're Not Supposed to Have Premarital Sex, Why Do Hormones Kick in So Early? ***Topic: Sex and Stuff*** (Side Two) . . . . 42 & 44

WHAT IS THIS?
Faith Conversations for Youth Peers
by Franklin W. Nelson

Editors: Jeffrey S. Nelson and Virginia Bonde Zarth
Cover design: David Meyer

Interior illustration: Studio Arts

ISBN 0-8066-4256-4

Manufactured in U.S.A.

05 04 03 02 01 1 2 3 4 5 6 7 8 9 10

A Message to Peers

Real Friendship

Have you noticed how much easier it is to talk with good friends about things that are important to you? That's because you are free to ask questions, say what's on your mind, give an opinion without wondering if your friend is going to reject you or put you down. This kind of friendship doesn't just happen. We have to do our part in building good friendship.

What Is This? is designed to help you do that with your peers (either one-on-one or in small groups of three or more). You will be guided in conversations about some of life's biggest questions. When you take the time to have the conversations in this book with your peers, you will soon discover a deeper friendship with your peers. You don't even need to agree with someone to be a friend, but you do need to listen and respect her or his viewpoint.

When you come to your church and become involved with your youth group, what do you expect? You probably want to learn more about God. You may want to have some of your questions about life answered. Almost everyone comes hoping to be accepted and loved by others. When you learn that God loves you unconditionally, you can be freer to love others in the same way—without strings attached. The talksheets in this book will guide you in conversations that will deepen your love for God and others.

What Are Your Questions?

That's what nearly 40,000 youth at a national gathering in St. Louis, Missouri, were asked. Their real questions were gathered from hundreds of sticky notes and sheets of paper. The questions were compiled and published in five little booklets called *Real Questions* (available through Augsburg Fortress at 1-800-328-4648), a great resource for youth groups.

What Is This? is based on the real questions of young people. You'll notice that the title for each of the conversations is a real question. In fact, this book is full of questions. In the conversations you and your peers will engage in, you will have a chance to ask some of your own questions.

Have you ever been around a two-year old who was full of questions? "What is that?" "Why?" "How does this work?" "What is this?" That's the way younger children learn about life, through their curiosity and questions. And that is also the way we all discover more and more about life. Our questions, even our doubts, can be the growing edge of knowledge and faith.

Did you know that Martin Luther wrote the Small Catechism when his oldest son, Hans, was a toddler? Hans followed his dad around the house and kept asking Luther, in German, *"Was ist das?"*—or in English, *"What is this?"* or *"What does this mean for us?"*

The *What Is This?* series of resources has been created to make it a lot easier for you to ask your own questions and have meaningful conversations with others about faith. Each talksheet will guide you in a process that is simple, open-ended, and makes it much easier to ask the questions and have the talks that will build your faith and friendship.

So, welcome, peers! Welcome to the experience of new friendships! Welcome to the continuing adventure of discovering what life and faith are about. Welcome to the joy of serving and sharing. Welcome to the spiritual growth you will enjoy as you enter into some very important conversations.

And thanks, peers! Thanks for your interest in the Christian faith and your involvement in these faith conversations.

Who Will Use What Is This?

You will soon discover that each talksheet in this book is duplicated, so that the book can be used in one-on-one relationships between youth peers of the same age or where an older youth will be meeting with a younger youth. The talksheets work well in small groups, too. Just order enough books so everyone has their own copy (one book for every two students—please do not photocopy the book). The faith conversations are ideal for confirmation programs, peer ministry programs, youth group discussions, Sunday school classes, youth retreats, and can even be picked up by two friends or two people in a dating relationship who want to deepen their friendship around topics of faith.

What Will I Find on Each Talksheet?

Each of the 10 talksheets has two related but separate topics, one on the front and one on the back. For example, you will find the topic of parents on side one of a talksheet and family on side two of that sheet. You may want to have a long conversation that covers both sides, or you may decide to use the one talksheet as two separate discussions. There are actually 20 topics of discussion within this resource, or 20 programs that can be topics used by youth groups.

The tear-out talksheets in this resource provide friends with a conversational map to follow. Remove the two copies of a particular talksheet so that each person has his or her own copy.

The conversation begins with a discussion about some of the real questions other young people are asking.

Next, a situation is presented and you are asked to talk about what you would do in that situation.

You'll need a pencil to write a response for each of the sentence completions in the center of each page.

Note: *The writing step is very important. Others who have used this communication process have found that it helps to have this time to think about what you want to say before you say it, so be sure to give it a try.*

When you're done writing, take turns talking about each response.

Take time to look up the scripture in your Bibles and discuss it.

Finally, there's a suggestion of something you can try to do in the coming week that relates in some way to what the topic is.

If there is time left, continue with Side 2 of the talksheet. If not, save Side 2 for another conversation.

Faith—What Is This?

Faith is all about healthy relationships with God, others, and self! Jesus said that the first and most important commandment is to "love the Lord your God with all your heart, and with all your soul, and with all your mind, and with all your strength" (Mark 12:30). If we love God with heart, mind, soul, and strength, the health of our relationship with God increases. The same is true in our relationships with others, even the relationship we have with our own self. So Jesus continues, "You shall love your neighbor [others] as yourself" (Mark 12:31).

Many times in the Bible, human beings are compared to trees. The prophet Jeremiah said that those who trust in the Lord "shall be like a tree planted by water, sending out its roots by the stream" (Jeremiah 17:8). And Jesus said, "every good tree bears good fruit, but the bad tree bears bad fruit . . . you will know [people of faith] by their fruits" (Matthew 7:17, 20).

If our lives are to be fruitful, we need to put down healthy roots in the soil of love. That means that our relationships with God, others, and self need to be full of love. That's why healthy, life-giving friendships, families, and youth groups are essential to the well-being of young people. Love gives us the roots we need to live healthy, fruitful lives.

Our baptism marks the beginning of a faith journey in which we are continually becoming more and more rooted in God's grace and love. A person who is "faith-full" is one who is developing a healthy root system in the soil of loving relationships with God, others, and self.

Choose, Help, Esteem, Know (CHEK)

Friends CHOOSE, HELP, ESTEEM, and KNOW each other more and more as their friendship grows. They "CHEK each other out."

C is for CHOOSE

Have you ever been invited to a party? Picked to play on a team? Chosen to be someone's special friend? It feels great to be chosen. In healthy relationships, we choose each other. We choose to spend time and to be involved. We choose to listen, care, love, support, and challenge. Even if we don't always like another person, we can still choose them anyway, because we are willing to take the time to look beyond their faults and get to know who they really are.

H is for HELP

When you need help from someone, it's great to have a person there who is willing to help you. And it's a good feeling to help others. Friendship depends on being willing to be in a relationship where we help each other. The Bible talks about our need to serve one another, and Jesus teaches, "whoever wishes to become great among you must be your servant" (Mark 10:43).

God has placed us in this world to help and serve one another, and when we do, friendship grows. Sometimes we may hurt each other, even in the best of relationships. But even then, we try to make it right again, because we're committed to making the friendship work.

E is for ESTEEM

Friends value and respect each other. The Bible uses the word *grace* to express this high level of esteem for others. In fact, esteem is so important that the Bible says, "For by grace you have been saved through faith, and this is not your own doing; it is the gift of God" (Ephesians 2:8). Over time we learn to accept and love another, and appreciate the other person's friendship deeply, because of grace. Grace-filled friendships are the best!

K is for KNOW

Friends know each other pretty well, because they have taken the time to choose, help, and esteem each other. It's more than just knowing some of the facts about another person. Friendship is learning to really understand the other person. The Bible teaches us that God knows us: "O Lord, you have searched me and known me. You know when I sit down and when I rise up; you discern my thoughts from far away" (Psalm 139:1, 2). One of the main goals of the spiritual life is to know God more and more.

When we CHEK each other out, and we CHOOSE, HELP, ESTEEM, and KNOW each other more and more, friendship and love grows; but healthy relationships don't grow overnight. Like trees planted in life-giving soil, this kind of growth happens when we are willing to create a history of choosing, helping, esteeming, and knowing.

To Love God

In our baptism God says "Yes!" to us. In confirmation, we hear God's "Yes!" in a powerful way and continue our lifelong journey of faith.

We **Choose** God, who long ago chose us. We **Help** God, who from the beginning has been helping us. We **Esteem** and value God, who has always esteemed and loved us, through our worship (worth-ship). And we see faith as a lifetime of growing to **Know** and understand the One who knows and understands each of us.

To Love Others

To love others in our families, schools, churches, neighborhoods, and world means that we have decided to relate to others as we would want them to relate to us. To love others is to Choose, Help, Esteem, and Know them.

To Love Myself

To love our own self means that we are learning to Choose, Help, Esteem, and Know ourselves as we develop and grow into the person God has created us to become.

The journey of life and faith, then, is an adventure of learning to love God more fully, love others more deeply, and love self more completely.

Good Communication

If we are to CHEK each other out and deepen our friendships, the single most important skill we need to learn is the skill of good communication. That's why you and your friend(s) are invited to communicate with the help of the talksheet guides in this resource. As you do, you will discover the joy of being a part of a relationship in which you are chosen, helped, esteemed, and known.

So, thanks for being willing to give the gift of your time and yourself to others. Thanks for being willing to communicate with others. Thanks for being willing to be a friend. And thanks for being willing to take a risk.

Where is God?

Copy One Side 1

How Would You Answer?

- If God created us, then who created God?
- Is doubting God a sin?
- Why did God create ticks and mosquitoes?
- Are we all worshiping the same God under different names?
- Why is God always thought of as male? Couldn't God just be God?

What Would You Do or Say?

If one of your friends told you they no longer believe that God even exists, how would you respond?

My Thoughts about God

Write a response to each of the following:

1. This is how I'd describe God (using words, a drawing, or both):

2. Here are three things I believe about God:

3. Here are three things I don't believe about God:

4. This is what I believe about Jesus Christ:

5. I doubt that God . . .

6. A person who has helped me understand more about God is . . .

7. If God had a question for me, this might be it:

What Does the Bible Say?

Find Genesis 1:1 and John 1:1 in the Bible. How do we discover more about God?

Try This

In the coming week try to start (or end) your day by talking with God using this three-part prayer:

1. God, I praise you for . . .
2. God, I thank you for . . .
3. God, today (or tomorrow) please help me to . . .

___ Yes, I'll give it a try in the coming week.

Why Are There So Many Religions?

How Would You Answer?

- What difference does faith make in a person's life?
- How do you connect with someone who feels confused about his or her faith?
- Why are there so many religions that contradict each other, but everybody believes they are right?
- Are we all worshiping the same God under different names?
- If churches of different denominations are all Christian, why do we slam each other?

What Would You Do or Say?

If you were dating a person (and liked that person a lot), then discovered that she or he was devoted to a non-Christian religion, would you continue the dating relationship? Why or why not?

My Thoughts about the Church

Write a response to each of the following:

1. Three positive words that describe my church are:

2. My church has helped me to . . .

3. I have helped my church by . . .

4. I think it's important to be an active part of a church because . . .

5. I wish my church would . . .

6. If I was talking to a friend who was in need of a church, I'd recommend my church because . . .

7. One question I have about my church is . .

8. My prayer for the church is: Dear God, . . .

What Does the Bible Say?

Read Acts 2:43-47 and list some of the characteristics of the early church that made it so attractive to people. Which of these characteristics describe your own church?

Try This

Interview (by phone, e-mail, or in person) an adult member of your church. Ask them some of the same questions from the list above.

___ Yes, I'll give it a try in the coming week.

Where is God?

Copy Two Side 1

How Would You Answer?

- If God created us, then who created God?
- Is doubting God a sin?
- Why did God create ticks and mosquitoes?
- Are we all worshiping the same God under different names?
- Why is God always thought of as male? Couldn't God just be God?

What Would You Do or Say?

If one of your friends told you they no longer believe that God even exists, how would you respond?

My Thoughts about God

Write a response to each of the following:

1. This is how I'd describe God (using words, a drawing, or both):

2. Here are three things I believe about God:

3. Here are three things I don't believe about God:

4. This is what I believe about Jesus Christ:

5. I doubt that God . . .

6. A person who has helped me understand more about God is . . .

7. If God had a question for me, this might be it:

What Does the Bible Say?

Find Genesis 1:1 and John 1:1 in the Bible. How do we discover more about God?

Try This

In the coming week try to start (or end) your day by talking with God using this three-part prayer:

1. God, I praise you for . . .
2. God, I thank you for . . .
3. God, today (or tomorrow) please help me to . . .

___ Yes, I'll give it a try in the coming week.

Why Are There So Many Religions?

Copy Two Side 2

How Would You Answer?

- What difference does faith make in a person's life?
- How do you connect with someone who feels confused about his or her faith?
- Why are there so many religions that contradict each other, but everybody believes they are right?
- Are we all worshiping the same God under different names?
- If churches of different denominations are all Christian, why do we slam each other?

What Would You Do or Say?

If you were dating a person (and liked that person a lot), then discovered that she or he was devoted to a non-Christian religion, would you continue the dating relationship? Why or why not?

My Thoughts about the Church

Write a response to each of the following:

1. Three positive words that describe my church are:

2. My church has helped me to . . .

3. I have helped my church by . . .

4. I think it's important to be an active part of a church because . . .

5. I wish my church would . . .

6. If I was talking to a friend who was in need of a church, I'd recommend my church because . . .

7. One question I have about my church is . .

8. My prayer for the church is: Dear God, . . .

What Does the Bible Say?

Read Acts 2:43-47 and list some of the characteristics of the early church that made it so attractive to people. Which of these characteristics describe your own church?

Try This

Interview (by phone, e-mail, or in person) an adult member of your church. Ask them some of the same questions from the list above.

___ Yes, I'll give it a try in the coming week.

Why Are Parents So Annoying?

Copy One Side 1

How Would You Answer?

- Why are parents so controlling?
- Why are parents so protective?
- Why do I always feel I have to scream at my parents to be heard?
- Why do adults not listen and not understand?
- Why do kids hate some stepparents?

What Would You Do or Say?

If you were the parent or guardian of a young person who came home 15 minutes past curfew on a Friday night, what would you do or say?

My Own Parents or Guardians

Write a response to each of the following:

1. Three words that describe my mom, stepmom, or guardian are:

2. Three words that describe my dad, stepdad, or guardian are:

3. I sometimes wonder why my parent(s) or guardian(s) . . .

4. I'm thankful that my parent(s) or guardian(s) seem willing to . . .

5. I sometimes wish my parent(s) or guardian(s) would try to understand that . . .

6. If I'm ever a parent or guardian, I hope that I'll take time with my children to . . .

What Does the Bible Say?

Look up Ephesians 6:1-3 and talk about what it means to honor or respect your parent(s) or guardian(s). Why do you think that honoring parents is important to God?

Try This

Go to a card shop and pick out a card that honors and expresses thanks to your parent(s) or guardian(s). Or just write a note that lists some things you appreciate about your parent(s) or guardian(s).

___ Yes, I'll give it a try in the coming week.

Why Do I Fight So Much with My Siblings? Copy One Side 2

How Would You Answer?

- Why am I in constant conflict with my family?
- Why don't families stick together?
- Why do I fight so much with my siblings?
- What makes a marriage last?
- Why did my parents split up?

What Would You Do or Say?

Situation 1: If you know the parents of one of your friends have separated and are planning to get a divorce, what would you do or say to help your friend?

Situation 2: Your brother (or sister) keeps borrowing your stuff and not returning it. Now he or she has broken something valuable to you. What would you do or say?

My Own Family

Write a response to each of the following:

1. Three words that describe my family are . . .

2. List each person in your family and two or three words describing the relationship you have with that person.

3. I enjoy it when my whole family . . .

4. The person in my family I feel closest to is . . .

5. I wish my brother(s) or sister(s) would . . .

6. I don't enjoy it when my family . . .

7. I wish my family spent more time . . .

8. One question I'd like to ask my family is:

9. I think God wants my family to be more . . .

What Does the Bible Say?

Read Ephesians 3:14-15 and talk about what you think the verse means.

Try This

Option 1: During the next seven days, do at least one kind, generous, helpful act for each member of your family.

Option 2: Initiate something your family enjoys doing together.

___ Yes, I'll give one of these a try in the coming week.

Why Are Parents So Annoying?

Copy Two Side 1

How Would You Answer?

- Why are parents so controlling?
- Why are parents so protective?
- Why do I always feel I have to scream at my parents to be heard?
- Why do adults not listen and not understand?
- Why do kids hate some stepparents?

What Would You Do or Say?

If you were the parent or guardian of a young person who came home 15 minutes past curfew on a Friday night, what would you do or say?

My Own Parents or Guardians

Write a response to each of the following:

1. Three words that describe my mom, stepmom, or guardian are:

2. Three words that describe my dad, stepdad, or guardian are:

3. I sometimes wonder why my parent(s) or guardian(s) . . .

4. I'm thankful that my parent(s) or guardian(s) seem willing to . . .

5. I sometimes wish my parent(s) or guardian(s) would try to understand that . . .

6. If I'm ever a parent or guardian, I hope that I'll take time with my children to . . .

What Does the Bible Say?

Look up Ephesians 6:1-3 and talk about what it means to honor or respect your parent(s) or guardian(s). Why do you think that honoring parents is important to God?

Try This

Go to a card shop and pick out a card that honors and expresses thanks to your parent(s) or guardian(s). Or just write a note that lists some things you appreciate about your parent(s) or guardian(s).

___ Yes, I'll give it a try in the coming week.

Why Do I Fight So Much with My Siblings? Copy Two Side 2

How Would You Answer?

- Why am I in constant conflict with my family?
- Why don't families stick together?
- Why do I fight so much with my siblings?
- What makes a marriage last?
- Why did my parents split up?

What Would You Do or Say?

Situation 1: If you know the parents of one of your friends have separated and are planning to get a divorce, what would you do or say to help your friend?

Situation 2: Your brother (or sister) keeps borrowing your stuff and not returning it. Now he or she has broken something valuable to you. What would you do or say?

My Own Family

Write a response to each of the following:

1. Three words that describe my family are . . .

2. List each person in your family and two or three words describing the relationship you have with that person.

3. I enjoy it when my whole family . . .

4. The person in my family I feel closest to is . . .

5. I wish my brother(s) or sister(s) would . . .

6. I don't enjoy it when my family . . .

7. I wish my family spent more time . . .

8. One question I'd like to ask my family is:

9. I think God wants my family to be more . . .

What Does the Bible Say?

Read Ephesians 3:14-15 and talk about what you think the verse means.

Try This

Option 1: During the next seven days, do at least one kind, generous, helpful act for each member of your family.

Option 2: Initiate something your family enjoys doing together.

___ Yes, I'll give one of these a try in the coming week.

How Can I Learn to Control My Temper?

Copy One Side 1

How Would You Answer?

- Why do we all fight?
- Why are people mean?
- Why are people so rude?
- How can people be racist?
- How can I learn to control my temper?

What Would You Do or Say?

Situation 1: If someone yelled at you and called you a string of names, how would you react? What would you say or do?

Situation 2: A friend of yours has an anger problem. Your friend often loses control of her or his temper. What would you do to help your friend?

My Own Anger

Write a response to each of the following:

1. I sometimes get angry when . . .

2. A person who sometimes makes me mad is . . .

3. I lost my temper once when . . .

4. Anger is a choice. Nobody can "make you mad." You can choose to not be angry.

__ I agree __ I disagree

because . . .

5. Instead of being angry at ______________ I wish I could choose instead to . . .

6. Jesus said, "Love your enemies." I think that's hard for me to do when my enemy . . .

7. I confess that I hate people who . . .

8. I think I have some prejudice against people who are . . .

What Does the Bible Say?

According to Romans 12:14-21, how are we to act toward people we may dislike or even hate?

Try This

Option 1: The next time you feel really mad at someone, take a deep breath, quiet yourself, count to 10, collect yourself, then respond.

Option 2: During the next seven days, each time you have a hateful or prejudiced thought or feeling toward someone (anyone), notice the thought, admit it to God, and seek God's forgiveness and love.

___ Yes, I'll give it a try in the coming week.

Why Do People Fight Over Silly Things?

Copy One Side 2

How Would You Answer?

- How do you get along with someone you don't like?
- Why didn't God take more action during the Holocaust?
- Why do people think violence solves problems better than words?
- Can't we all just get along?
- Is war ever justified?

What Would You Do or Say?

If you had a major conflict or fight with someone (in your family, at school, at church, or with a friend) and you tried to talk with the person about it, but that person wouldn't listen, what might be a next step?

My Own Thoughts about Conflict

Write a response to each of the following:

Step 1: Describe a problem, issue, or disagreement you have with a person that is still unresolved.

Step 2: Identify the most significant feelings you have about this conflict:

angry ignored stubborn confused open frustrated guilty weak depressed foolish hopeless afraid discouraged

Step 3: [to be done with the other person(s)]: Before you continue, agree on the issue and talk about your feelings.

Step 4: Think of what could be done to help the situation:
I could improve this situation if I would . . .

It would help if the other person(s) would . . .

Step 5: Decide one thing you both can and will do to improve the situation:
To make things better, I'm willing to . . .

I expect us both to be willing to . . .

We'll know there's been positive change when . . .

What Does the Bible Say?

Look up Matthew 18:15-17 and talk about the guideline Jesus gives for resolving our conflicts. Why is it difficult to resolve conflict in this way (face-to-face)?

Try This

If it's appropriate, use the above steps to resolve a conflict or tension you may have right now with someone. Look at the Bible verses with the other person, then talk together about each of the steps listed, with the goal of resolving the conflict.

___ Yes, I'll give it a try in the coming week.

How Can I Learn to Control My Temper?

Copy Two Side 1

How Would You Answer?

- Why do we all fight?
- Why are people mean?
- Why are people so rude?
- How can people be racist?
- How can I learn to control my temper?

What Would You Do or Say?

Situation 1: If someone yelled at you and called you a string of names, how would you react? What would you say or do?

Situation 2: A friend of yours has an anger problem. Your friend often loses control of her or his temper. What would you do to help your friend?

My Own Anger

Write a response to each of the following:

1. I sometimes get angry when . . .

2. A person who sometimes makes me mad is . . .

3. I lost my temper once when . . .

4. Anger is a choice. Nobody can "make you mad." You can choose to not be angry.

__ I agree __ I disagree

because . . .

5. Instead of being angry at _______________ I wish I could choose instead to . . .

6. Jesus said, "Love your enemies." I think that's hard for me to do when my enemy . . .

7. I confess that I hate people who . . .

8. I think I have some prejudice against people who are . . .

What Does the Bible Say?

According to Romans 12:14-21, how are we to act toward people we may dislike or even hate?

Try This

Option 1: The next time you feel really mad at someone, take a deep breath, quiet yourself, count to 10, collect yourself, then respond.

Option 2: During the next seven days, each time you have a hateful or prejudiced thought or feeling toward someone (anyone), notice the thought, admit it to God, and seek God's forgiveness and love.

___ Yes, I'll give it a try in the coming week.

Why Do People Fight Over Silly Things?

Copy Two Side 2

How Would You Answer?

- How do you get along with someone you don't like?
- Why didn't God take more action during the Holocaust?
- Why do people think violence solves problems better than words?
- Can't we all just get along?
- Is war ever justified?

What Would You Do or Say?

If you had a major conflict or fight with someone (in your family, at school, at church, or with a friend) and you tried to talk with the person about it, but that person wouldn't listen, what might be a next step?

My Own Thoughts about Conflict

Write a response to each of the following:

Step 1: Describe a problem, issue, or disagreement you have with a person that is still unresolved.

Step 2: Identify the most significant feelings you have about this conflict:

angry ignored stubborn confused open frustrated guilty weak depressed foolish hopeless afraid discouraged

Step 3: [to be done with the other person(s)]: Before you continue, agree on the issue and talk about your feelings.

Step 4: Think of what could be done to help the situation:
I could improve this situation if I would . . .

It would help if the other person(s) would . . .

Step 5: Decide one thing you both can and will do to improve the situation:
To make things better, I'm willing to . . .

I expect us both to be willing to . . .

We'll know there's been positive change when . . .

What Does the Bible Say?

Look up Matthew 18:15-17 and talk about the guideline Jesus gives for resolving our conflicts. Why is it difficult to resolve conflict in this way (face-to-face)?

Try This

If it's appropriate, use the above steps to resolve a conflict or tension you may have right now with someone. Look at the Bible verses with the other person, then talk together about each of the steps listed, with the goal of resolving the conflict.

___ Yes, I'll give it a try in the coming week.

Does God Have a Specific Purpose for Me?

Copy One Side 1

How Would You Answer?

- Some say we choose our own path, but some say God has a plan for you. Which is it?
- Why is it hard to face the future?
- When will I find true love, and how will I know when I do?
- How will I know when I've found myself?
- Is there such a thing as fate?

What Would You Do or Say?

If your teacher assigned you to write an essay on three things you want to accomplish in your lifetime, what would be three things you might write about?

Thoughts about My Future

Write a response to each of the following:

1. In the future . . .

I want to learn how to . . .

I'd like to travel to . . .

I'd like to be able to experience . . .

I'd like to become a person who . . .

2. When I think about the future, I feel . . .

(very pessimistic) 1 2 3 4 5 6 7 8 (very optimistic)

because . . .

3. Sometimes when I think about the future, I fear . . .

4. One question I have about the future is . . .

5. A question God might want to ask me about my future is . . .

What Does the Bible Say?

Read Hebrews 12:1-2 and talk about the part faith can play in helping us look forward to the future.

Try This

Pray first, then try to write a paragraph describing "My Life's Main Purpose or Goal." Attach the paper to your mirror or slip it in your Bible for safekeeping. As you continue to mature, make any necessary changes in the months and years ahead.

___ Yes, I'll give it a try in the coming week.

Why Is School So Boring?

How Would You Answer?

- Why is there a big obsession with going to college right after high school?
- When will I use what they teach me in school?
- Why can't the school day start at noon?
- Why do teenagers form cliques in school?
- Why do we have to go to school?

What Would You Do or Say?

It's summer and you've just graduated from high school. You have plans to continue your education in the fall, but your two best friends have invited you to take the year off and go out West to find jobs and a place to stay in the mountains. What would you do? Say?

My Thoughts about Education

Write a response to each of the following:

1. One of my favorite teachers was or is . . . because he or she . . .

2. I sometimes have trouble in school with . . .

3. Interests or subjects I like most include . . .

4. I'd describe myself as . . .

(a poor student) 1 2 3 4 5 6 7 8 (an excellent student)

because . . .

5. If a child asked me, "Why is it so important for me to go to school?" I'd say . . .

6. Finishing high school is important for me because . . .

7. I believe education beyond high school is important, because it will help me to . . .

8. A prayer for my educational future is: Dear God, help me to . . .

What Does the Bible Say?

See what Ecclesiastes 7:23-25 has to say, and then discuss what you think *wisdom* is. How does one find it? What is the relationship between study and wisdom?

Try This

Option 1: Think of three things you would like to know more about. Choose one. Then, using the Internet, a library, or encyclopedia, spend 30 minutes researching the subject.

Option 2: For one week read the front page of the newspaper (if your family gets the paper) or watch the evening news. Try to become more aware of what is going on in the world around you, and think about the news and events with a critical mind.

___ Yes, I'll give it a try in the coming week.

Does God Have a Specific Purpose for Me?

Copy Two Side 1

How Would You Answer?

- Some say we choose our own path, but some say God has a plan for you. Which is it?
- Why is it hard to face the future?
- When will I find true love, and how will I know when I do?
- How will I know when I've found myself?
- Is there such a thing as fate?

What Would You Do or Say?

If your teacher assigned you to write an essay on three things you want to accomplish in your lifetime, what would be three things you might write about?

Thoughts about My Future

Write a response to each of the following:

1. In the future . . .

I want to learn how to . . .

I'd like to travel to . . .

I'd like to be able to experience . . .

I'd like to become a person who . . .

2. When I think about the future, I feel . . .

(very pessimistic) 1 2 3 4 5 6 7 8 (very optimistic)

because . . .

3. Sometimes when I think about the future, I fear . . .

4. One question I have about the future is . . .

5. A question God might want to ask me about my future is . . .

What Does the Bible Say?

Read Hebrews 12:1-2 and talk about the part faith can play in helping us look forward to the future.

Try This

Pray first, then try to write a paragraph describing "My Life's Main Purpose or Goal." Attach the paper to your mirror or slip it in your Bible for safekeeping. As you continue to mature, make any necessary changes in the months and years ahead.

___ Yes, I'll give it a try in the coming week.

Why Is School So Boring?

Copy Two Side 2

How Would You Answer?

- Why is there a big obsession with going to college right after high school?
- When will I use what they teach me in school?
- Why can't the school day start at noon?
- Why do teenagers form cliques in school?
- Why do we have to go to school?

What Would You Do or Say?

It's summer and you've just graduated from high school. You have plans to continue your education in the fall, but your two best friends have invited you to take the year off and go out West to find jobs and a place to stay in the mountains. What would you do? Say?

My Thoughts about Education

Write a response to each of the following:

1. One of my favorite teachers was or is . . . because he or she . . .

2. I sometimes have trouble in school with . . .

3. Interests or subjects I like most include . . .

4. I'd describe myself as . . .

(a poor student) 1 2 3 4 5 6 7 8 (an excellent student)

because . . .

5. If a child asked me, "Why is it so important for me to go to school?" I'd say . . .

6. Finishing high school is important for me because . . .

7. I believe education beyond high school is important, because it will help me to . . .

8. A prayer for my educational future is: Dear God, help me to . . .

What Does the Bible Say?

See what Ecclesiastes 7:23-25 has to say, and then discuss what you think *wisdom* is. How does one find it? What is the relationship between study and wisdom?

Try This

Option 1: Think of three things you would like to know more about. Choose one. Then, using the Internet, a library, or encyclopedia, spend 30 minutes researching the subject.

Option 2: For one week read the front page of the newspaper (if your family gets the paper) or watch the evening news. Try to become more aware of what is going on in the world around you, and think about the news and events with a critical mind.

___ Yes, I'll give it a try in the coming week.

Why Are There So Many Temptations in Life? Copy One Side 1

How Would You Answer?

- Is everyone forgiven by God—no matter what?
- Why do I do wrong things when I know they are wrong?
- Why are everyone's values so different?
- How big of a sin is it to have sex with a person you are not going to marry?
- Why is there such evil in the world?

What Would You Do or Say?

You're shopping with a friend in a store and you notice that your friend slips a CD into her or his pocket, then walks out the door without paying. What would you do or say? Why?

My Thoughts about Morality

Write a response to each of the following:

1. I think it's definitely wrong to . . .

2. In addition, I'm sure God doesn't want us to . . .

3. To receive God's forgiveness for something I've done means that I . . .

4. One of the biggest mistakes or sins I ever committed was the time I . . .

5. I believe God forgives us unconditionally.

yes, absolutely 1 2 3 4 5 6 7 8 no, not without something from me

Please explain:

6. To say "I'm a moral person" means that I . . .

7. To say that I'm an "immoral person" means that I . . .

8. Three behaviors I consider to be immoral include . . .

9. If someone asked me "Who decides what is moral and what is immoral?" I'd say . . .

What Does the Bible Say?

Read Romans 7:15 and talk about the battle inside us between doing what is right and doing what is wrong. What or who can help us? (See verses 24-25.)

Try This

In private, make a list of all the things you have done that you know were wrong and cause you to feel ashamed or guilty. Then, take the piece of paper and rip it up into little pieces, letting go of the shame and guilt. Prayerfully receive God's forgiveness.

___ Yes, I'll give it a try in the coming week.

What Makes a Good Decision?

Copy One Side 2

How Would You Answer?

- Is it okay if I marry someone of a different race?
- Why do people make stupid decisions, fully aware of the consequences?
- What is the benefit of marriage if so many of them end in divorce?
- Why should I believe in God?
- Is it okay if I listen to music that represents Satanism, but still believe in God?

What Would You Do or Say?

Discuss these simple choices. Which would you choose? Ice cream or pizza? Going to a movie or watching a video at home? Internet surfing or going to the library? A box of cereal or a box of chocolates? A waffle or a pancake? Doing what you want to do or doing what you believe God wants you to do?

My Own Choices

Write a response to each of the following:

1. Five choices I have made since I woke up this morning:

2. One of my best choices was the time I decided to . . .

3. One of my worst (or most embarrassing) choices was the time I . . .

4. An example of a time when I felt pressured by someone to do something I knew was wrong was . . .

5. When I need to make a wise choice, I find it helpful to take the time to . . .

6. One person I know and trust who would help me if I had a difficult decision to make is . . .

7. The choices we make determine our future and who we become.

___ I agree ___ I disagree

because . . .

What Does the Bible Say?

Look up Deuteronomy 30:19-20 and talk about what it means to choose life rather than death. What does it mean to choose to live for God rather than for ourselves?

Try This

For the next seven days, pray at bedtime, thanking God for the wisdom God gave you for a wise choice you made that day, and receiving God's forgiveness for a poor choice you made.

___ Yes, I'll give it a try in the coming week.

Why Are There So Many Temptations in Life? Copy Two Side 1

How Would You Answer?

- Is everyone forgiven by God—no matter what?
- Why do I do wrong things when I know they are wrong?
- Why are everyone's values so different?
- How big of a sin is it to have sex with a person you are not going to marry?
- Why is there such evil in the world?

What Would You Do or Say?

You're shopping with a friend in a store and you notice that your friend slips a CD into her or his pocket, then walks out the door without paying. What would you do or say? Why?

My Thoughts about Morality

Write a response to each of the following:

1. I think it's definitely wrong to . . .

2. In addition, I'm sure God doesn't want us to . . .

3. To receive God's forgiveness for something I've done means that I . . .

4. One of the biggest mistakes or sins I ever committed was the time I . . .

5. I believe God forgives us unconditionally.

yes, absolutely 1 2 3 4 5 6 7 8 no, not without something from me

Please explain:

6. To say "I'm a moral person" means that I . . .

7. To say that I'm an "immoral person" means that I . . .

8. Three behaviors I consider to be immoral include . . .

9. If someone asked me "Who decides what is moral and what is immoral?" I'd say . . .

What Does the Bible Say?

Read Romans 7:15 and talk about the battle inside us between doing what is right and doing what is wrong. What or who can help us? (See verses 24-25.)

Try This

In private, make a list of all the things you have done that you know were wrong and cause you to feel ashamed or guilty. Then, take the piece of paper and rip it up into little pieces, letting go of the shame and guilt. Prayerfully receive God's forgiveness.

___ Yes, I'll give it a try in the coming week.

What Makes a Good Decision?

Copy Two Side 2

How Would You Answer?

- Is it okay if I marry someone of a different race?
- Why do people make stupid decisions, fully aware of the consequences?
- What is the benefit of marriage if so many of them end in divorce?
- Why should I believe in God?
- Is it okay if I listen to music that represents Satanism, but still believe in God?

What Would You Do or Say?

Discuss these simple choices. Which would you choose? Ice cream or pizza? Going to a movie or watching a video at home? Internet surfing or going to the library? A box of cereal or a box of chocolates? A waffle or a pancake? Doing what you want to do or doing what you believe God wants you to do?

My Own Choices

Write a response to each of the following:

1. Five choices I have made since I woke up this morning:

2. One of my best choices was the time I decided to . . .

3. One of my worst (or most embarrassing) choices was the time I . . .

4. An example of a time when I felt pressured by someone to do something I knew was wrong was . . .

5. When I need to make a wise choice, I find it helpful to take the time to . . .

6. One person I know and trust who would help me if I had a difficult decision to make is . . .

7. The choices we make determine our future and who we become.

___ I agree ___ I disagree

because . . .

What Does the Bible Say?

Look up Deuteronomy 30:19-20 and talk about what it means to choose life rather than death. What does it mean to choose to live for God rather than for ourselves?

Try This

For the next seven days, pray at bedtime, thanking God for the wisdom God gave you for a wise choice you made that day, and receiving God's forgiveness for a poor choice you made.

___ Yes, I'll give it a try in the coming week.

Why Are Young People Using Drugs and Alcohol? Copy One Side 1

How Would You Answer?

- What does God think when he sees people doing drugs?
- Why is marijuana illegal and frowned upon while alcohol is legal and socially acceptable?
- Why do people turn to drugs?
- What does the Bible have to say about alcohol and about faith?
- Is it bad to drink alcohol?

What Would You Do or Say?

You're watching a video with one of your best friends when your friend pulls a six-pack of beer from the fridge and invites you to have one. What would you do? Say? Feel? Why?

My Own Stand on Drugs and Alcohol

Write a response to each of the following:

1. In our state a person has to be ___ years of age to purchase alcohol legally. What is the reason for that law?

2. Three reasons I might choose to drink alcohol include . . .

3. Three reasons I might choose to say no to alcohol include . . .

4. If one of my friends offered me an illegal drug and said "Try it, just once!" I'd probably . . .

5. This is what my parents have taught me (by their own example) about alcohol:

6. If a friend of mine had a drinking problem, I would try to help by . . .

7. One question I have about drugs and alcohol is . . .

8. When God sees young people drinking alcohol or using drugs, I think God . . .

What Does the Bible Say?

Find Proverbs 20:1 in the Bible and talk about the advice this verse gives for those who are wondering if it is a good idea to drink alcohol.

Try This

Make a commitment to yourself and at least one other person, from this day forward, to stay completely free of mood-altering drugs, including alcohol, marijuana, and other illegal drugs until you are of legal age. Revisit this commitment when you are of legal age. Write your commitment on a piece of paper and keep it in a safe place.

__ Yes, I'll give it a try in the coming week.

Is Smoking Going to Kill Me?

Copy One Side 2

How Would You Answer?

- Shouldn't marijuana be legal?
- Is smoking going to kill me?
- Why do people smoke?
- Why do parents tell you not to smoke, do drugs, and drink but they do it themselves?
- Why is life so full of tests?

What Would You Do or Say?

A good friend of yours thinks he or she might be addicted to nicotine and can't seem to quit smoking. How might you help? Where can your friend go to find the help he or she needs?

My Own Thoughts about Smoking

Write a response to each of the following:

1. Some of the main reasons people choose to start smoking cigarettes include . . .

2. The main reasons never to start include . . .

3. I think there has been a growing number of young people smoking because . . .

4. Smoking cigarettes can easily lead to smoking pot. ___ I agree ___ I disagree

because . . .

5. A close friend offers you a cigarette and says "Just try it once! It'll make you feel better." You'd say . . .

6. If it's a choice between smoking and not smoking, I think God would want me to choose . . .

for these reasons:

What Does the Bible Say?

Read 1 Corinthians 3:16-17. Discuss the verses. Does the message here give any advice on smoking?

Try This

Make a commitment to yourself and at least one other person, from this day forward, to stay away completely from tobacco products for the rest of your life. If you already use tobacco, decide today to quit and seek help if you are addicted. Write your commitment on a piece of paper and keep it in a safe place.

___ Yes, I'll give it a try in the coming week.

Why Are Young People Using Drugs and Alcohol? Copy Two Side 1

How Would You Answer?

- What does God think when he sees people doing drugs?
- Why is marijuana illegal and frowned upon while alcohol is legal and socially acceptable?
- Why do people turn to drugs?
- What does the Bible have to say about alcohol and about faith?
- Is it bad to drink alcohol?

What Would You Do or Say?

You're watching a video with one of your best friends when your friend pulls a six-pack of beer from the fridge and invites you to have one. What would you do? Say? Feel? Why?

My Own Stand on Drugs and Alcohol

Write a response to each of the following:

1. In our state a person has to be ___ years of age to purchase alcohol legally. What is the reason for that law?

2. Three reasons I might choose to drink alcohol include . . .

3. Three reasons I might choose to say no to alcohol include . . .

4. If one of my friends offered me an illegal drug and said "Try it, just once!" I'd probably . . .

5. This is what my parents have taught me (by their own example) about alcohol:

6. If a friend of mine had a drinking problem, I would try to help by . . .

7. One question I have about drugs and alcohol is . . .

8. When God sees young people drinking alcohol or using drugs, I think God . . .

What Does the Bible Say?

Find Proverbs 20:1 in the Bible and talk about the advice this verse gives for those who are wondering if it is a good idea to drink alcohol.

Try This

Make a commitment to yourself and at least one other person, from this day forward, to stay completely free of mood-altering drugs, including alcohol, marijuana, and other illegal drugs until you are of legal age. Revisit this commitment when you are of legal age. Write your commitment on a piece of paper and keep it in a safe place.

__ Yes, I'll give it a try in the coming week.

Is Smoking Going to Kill Me?

How Would You Answer?

- Shouldn't marijuana be legal?
- Is smoking going to kill me?
- Why do people smoke?
- Why do parents tell you not to smoke, do drugs, and drink but they do it themselves?
- Why is life so full of tests?

What Would You Do or Say?

A good friend of yours thinks he or she might be addicted to nicotine and can't seem to quit smoking. How might you help? Where can your friend go to find the help he or she needs?

My Own Thoughts about Smoking

Write a response to each of the following:

1. Some of the main reasons people choose to start smoking cigarettes include . . .

2. The main reasons never to start include . . .

3. I think there has been a growing number of young people smoking because . . .

4. Smoking cigarettes can easily lead to smoking pot. ___ I agree ___ I disagree

because . . .

5. A close friend offers you a cigarette and says "Just try it once! It'll make you feel better." You'd say . . .

6. If it's a choice between smoking and not smoking, I think God would want me to choose . . .

for these reasons:

What Does the Bible Say?

Read 1 Corinthians 3:16-17. Discuss the verses. Does the message here give any advice on smoking?

Try This

Make a commitment to yourself and at least one other person, from this day forward, to stay away completely from tobacco products for the rest of your life. If you already use tobacco, decide today to quit and seek help if you are addicted. Write your commitment on a piece of paper and keep it in a safe place.

___ Yes, I'll give it a try in the coming week.

Who Decides What Popular Is?

Copy One Side 1

How Would You Answer?

- Why are we upset with our bodies, which are God's creation?
- Why does everyone go through the "I hate myself and I am ugly" phase?
- Why can't I ever get it through my head that I am worth loving?
- What is normal?
- What kind of society makes young girls hate their bodies?
- Why do people feel they need to be beautiful to be liked?

What Would You Do or Say?

Someone you respect and like, who knows you well, says to you, "Did you know you're ugly?" How would you react? Feel? What would you say or do about it?

My Own Image

Write a response to each of the following:

1. Three positive words that describe me are:

2. Three negative words that describe me are:

3. One thing I like about myself is . . .

4. One thing I don't like about myself is . . .

5. I am sometimes too hard on myself when it comes to . . .

6. I feel really good about myself when . . .

7. A person who helps me feel good about myself is __________ because she or he . . .

8. I believe God thinks I am . . .

9. My prayer is: Dear God, help me to . . .

What Does the Bible Say?

Read Genesis 1:26 and talk about what you believe it means to be created in the image or likeness of God. Also read Mark 12:30-31 and discuss what it means to love yourself.

Try This

Take any magazine and page through it looking for images and messages defining our culture's view of who is beautiful or attractive. Look up the word *beauty* in a dictionary and think about ways you could become more beautiful in the eyes of God, others, and yourself.

___ Yes, I'll give it a try in the coming week.

Why Is Life So Difficult?

Copy One Side 2

How Would You Answer?

- How can I quit worrying and stop stress?
- Why is there so much pressure on teens today? Do adults realize it?
- Are teen years some of the hardest to live through?
- Why is growing up so difficult?
- Why do I feel God is not there in the times when I need God most?

What Would You Do or Say?

You've come to a time in your life when you are stressed out by school activities, homework, parents, friends, and a part-time job. What might you do to relieve your stress?

My Own Stress Level

Write a response to each of the following:

1. Name one thing that can cause stress in these areas of life:

Family:

School:

Work:

Money:

Friends:

2. A person who "stresses me out" is . . .

because he or she . . .

3. This is what I'm like when I'm stressed out:

4. When I feel stressed, it helps me to take time to . . .

5. When I'm stressed it helps me to know that God . . .

6. In the future I'd like to learn to handle my stress better by . . .

What Does the Bible Say?

Read Psalm 23 and talk about some of the images in the psalm that can help us with our stress. How can a healthy spiritual life help us to deal with the many challenges and stresses of life?

Try This

Next time you are stressed, name some of the things that are causing you to feel that way, press the "pause button," count to 10 (or 20), breathe deeply, and pray. Try to entrust stressful things to God and seek God's strength and peace.

___ Yes, I'll give it a try in the coming week.

Who Decides What Popular Is?

Copy Two Side 1

How Would You Answer?

- Why are we upset with our bodies, which are God's creation?
- Why does everyone go through the "I hate myself and I am ugly" phase?
- Why can't I ever get it through my head that I am worth loving?
- What is normal?
- What kind of society makes young girls hate their bodies?
- Why do people feel they need to be beautiful to be liked?

What Would You Do or Say?

Someone you respect and like, who knows you well, says to you, "Did you know you're ugly?" How would you react? Feel? What would you say or do about it?

My Own Image

Write a response to each of the following:

1. Three positive words that describe me are:
2. Three negative words that describe me are:
3. One thing I like about myself is . . .
4. One thing I don't like about myself is . . .
5. I am sometimes too hard on myself when it comes to . . .
6. I feel really good about myself when . . .
7. A person who helps me feel good about myself is __________ because she or he . . .
8. I believe God thinks I am . . .
9. My prayer is: Dear God, help me to . . .

What Does the Bible Say?

Read Genesis 1:26 and talk about what you believe it means to be created in the image or likeness of God. Also read Mark 12:30-31 and discuss what it means to love yourself.

Try This

Take any magazine and page through it looking for images and messages defining our culture's view of who is beautiful or attractive. Look up the word *beauty* in a dictionary and think about ways you could become more beautiful in the eyes of God, others, and yourself.

___ Yes, I'll give it a try in the coming week.

Why Is Life So Difficult?

Copy Two Side 2

How Would You Answer?

- How can I quit worrying and stop stress?
- Why is there so much pressure on teens today? Do adults realize it?
- Are teen years some of the hardest to live through?
- Why is growing up so difficult?
- Why do I feel God is not there in the times when I need God most?

What Would You Do or Say?

You've come to a time in your life when you are stressed out by school activities, homework, parents, friends, and a part-time job. What might you do to relieve your stress?

My Own Stress Level

Write a response to each of the following:

1. Name one thing that can cause stress in these areas of life:

Family:

School:

Work:

Money:

Friends:

2. A person who "stresses me out" is . . .

because he or she . . .

3. This is what I'm like when I'm stressed out:

4. When I feel stressed, it helps me to take time to . . .

5. When I'm stressed it helps me to know that God . . .

6. In the future I'd like to learn to handle my stress better by . . .

What Does the Bible Say?

Read Psalm 23 and talk about some of the images in the psalm that can help us with our stress. How can a healthy spiritual life help us to deal with the many challenges and stresses of life?

Try This

Next time you are stressed, name some of the things that are causing you to feel that way, press the "pause button," count to 10 (or 20), breathe deeply, and pray. Try to entrust stressful things to God and seek God's strength and peace.

___ Yes, I'll give it a try in the coming week.

What Is a True Friend?

Copy One Side 1

How Would You Answer?

- Why are people, especially teens, so mean to each other?
- What is a true friend?
- Does everyone have a soul mate?
- Why aren't people friendly in today's society?
- Do I fit in? What if I don't?

What Would You Do or Say?

Situation 1: You have recently moved to a new community and don't know a single soul. In order to make some new friends, what are some things you would do?

Situation 2: A close friend of yours thinks she or he has an eating disorder, but she or he has not yet gone for help. What can you say or do to help your friend?

My Own Friends

Write a response to each of the following:

1. Some of my childhood friends included . . .

2. And some of the things we enjoyed doing together included . . .

3. Among my best friends now are (list names) . . .

4. And some of the things we like to do together include . . .

5. A true friend is a person who . . .

6. Qualities I look for in choosing my friends include . . .

7. Things that can quickly ruin a good friendship are . . .

8. My prayer is: Dear God, in my friendships, help me to . . .

What Does the Bible Say?

Look up John 15:12-17 and talk about the kind of friend Jesus wants to be to us. What are some ways we can develop our friendship with Jesus?

Try This

Think about a person who has few (or no) friends. In the next few days do something friendly with or for that person.

___ Yes, I'll give it a try in the coming week.

Why Do People Care If They Are Popular?

Copy One Side 2

How Would You Answer?

- Why do so many teens stress out about being different?
- How can we follow the crowd and still do the right thing?
- Why don't kids feel comfortable talking to each other about God?
- Why are people always afraid of what other people think of them?
- Why do we tend to exclude those who are different?

What Would You Do or Say?

It's Halloween and your friends have invited you to make some mischief in the neighborhood, but you really don't want to go with them. They say, "Aw, come on, it'll be a lot of fun!" What do you say? Do? How do you handle the situation without losing your self-respect or your friendships?

My Own Thoughts about Peer Pressure

Write a response to each of the following:

1. To be popular in my school, it seems to help if you . . .

dress this way:

look this way (physically):

are involved in these activities:

get these grades:

use this kind of language:

on the weekends are willing to:

2. If I talked about God or the church with my friends at school, they would probably think I was . . .

3. It's hard or easy for me to stand up for what I believe if it goes against the crowd, because . . .

4. I felt peer pressure to do something I didn't want to do when . . .

This is how I handled it:

5. The reasons people want to be well-liked and accepted by their peers include . . .

What Does the Bible Say?

Read Romans 12:1-2 and talk about it. What does it mean to be conformed to the world? What does it mean to discern God's will?

Try This

Next time you feel pressure from a friend to do something or say something you think is wrong for you, say no and give your reasons.

___ Yes, I'll try to do it.

What Is a True Friend?

Copy Two Side 1

How Would You Answer?

- Why are people, especially teens, so mean to each other?
- What is a true friend?
- Does everyone have a soul mate?
- Why aren't people friendly in today's society?
- Do I fit in? What if I don't?

What Would You Do or Say?

Situation 1: You have recently moved to a new community and don't know a single soul. In order to make some new friends, what are some things you would do?

Situation 2: A close friend of yours thinks she or he has an eating disorder, but she or he has not yet gone for help. What can you say or do to help your friend?

My Own Friends

Write a response to each of the following:

1. Some of my childhood friends included . . .

2. And some of the things we enjoyed doing together included . . .

3. Among my best friends now are (list names) . . .

4. And some of the things we like to do together include . . .

5. A true friend is a person who . . .

6. Qualities I look for in choosing my friends include . . .

7. Things that can quickly ruin a good friendship are . . .

8. My prayer is: Dear God, in my friendships, help me to . . .

What Does the Bible Say?

Look up John 15:12-17 and talk about the kind of friend Jesus wants to be to us. What are some ways we can develop our friendship with Jesus?

Try This

Think about a person who has few (or no) friends. In the next few days do something friendly with or for that person.

___ Yes, I'll give it a try in the coming week.

Why Do People Care If They Are Popular?

Copy Two Side 2

How Would You Answer?

- Why do so many teens stress out about being different?
- How can we follow the crowd and still do the right thing?
- Why don't kids feel comfortable talking to each other about God?
- Why are people always afraid of what other people think of them?
- Why do we tend to exclude those who are different?

What Would You Do or Say?

It's Halloween and your friends have invited you to make some mischief in the neighborhood, but you really don't want to go with them. They say, "Aw, come on, it'll be a lot of fun!" What do you say? Do? How do you handle the situation without losing your self-respect or your friendships?

My Own Thoughts about Peer Pressure

Write a response to each of the following:

1. To be popular in my school, it seems to help if you . . .

dress this way:

look this way (physically):

are involved in these activities:

get these grades:

use this kind of language:

on the weekends are willing to:

2. If I talked about God or the church with my friends at school, they would probably think I was . . .

3. It's hard or easy for me to stand up for what I believe if it goes against the crowd, because . . .

4. I felt peer pressure to do something I didn't want to do when . . .

This is how I handled it:

5. The reasons people want to be well-liked and accepted by their peers include . . .

What Does the Bible Say?

Read Romans 12:1-2 and talk about it. What does it mean to be conformed to the world? What does it mean to discern God's will?

Try This

Next time you feel pressure from a friend to do something or say something you think is wrong for you, say no and give your reasons.

____ Yes, I'll try to do it.

Why Did My Friend Die?

Copy One Side 1

How Would You Answer?

- How does God embrace those who take their own life?
- Why do people say that it was "God's plan" when someone dies?
- How do I get over the fear of my parents dying?
- How do I enroll for heaven?
- Do ghosts exist?

What Would You Do or Say?

You are in the hallway after the memorial service for a close friend or family member who has died. Someone approaches you to express their support and says, "It was God's will. When it's time for us to go, God takes us." How would you feel? What would you think? Say?

My Own Thoughts about Death

Write a response to each of the following:

1. One question I have about death is . . .

2. This is what I believe about life after death:

3. This is how I feel about my own death:

I have no fear 1 2 3 4 5 6 7 8 I'm afraid to die

because . . .

4. This is what I believe about heaven:

5. This is what I believe about hell:

6. This is what I believe about suicide:

7. This is what I believe about the importance of the death of Jesus on the cross:

8. This is what I believe about Easter and the resurrection of Jesus:

What Does the Bible Say?

Talk about 1 Thessalonians 4:13-14. How does our belief in Jesus Christ help us to understand the meaning of our own suffering and death?

Try This

Option 1: Take time to visit a funeral home near you. If possible, go with a friend or youth group. Ask the receptionist to give you information about preplanning a funeral. Is grief counseling offered by the funeral home?

Option 2: Interview your parent or guardian and ask that person about his or her thoughts on death and dying. Has that person made plans to prepare for his or her own death?

___ Yes, I'll give it a try in the coming week.

Why Do We Feel a Need to Cover Up Our Feelings? Copy One Side 2

How Would You Answer?

- How do I stop feeling depressed?
- Why don't guys show their emotions?
- Why aren't people clear about their feelings?
- Is worrying a sin?
- Does love always hurt?
- Is it normal to be so lonely all the time?

What Would You Do or Say?

Though you are able to cover it up well, you have a constant feeling of sadness inside you. You're wondering if you might be depressed. Who can you talk to? What would you say? If you are depressed and need to go to a doctor, whom would you go to?

My Own Feelings

Write a response to each of the following: Here is a list of a variety of feelings. For each one, think of a time when you felt that way:

1. I felt happy when . . .

2. I felt relieved when . . .

3. I felt ashamed when . . .

4. I felt sad when . . .

5. I felt joyful when . . .

6. I felt confused when . . .

7. I felt depressed when . . .

8. I felt embarrassed when . . .

9. I felt loved when . . .

What Does the Bible Say?

Read John 14:1 and discuss how believing in Jesus can help troubled hearts. In addition, look at Romans 5:1-5 and talk about the advice Paul gives to those who are troubled and suffering.

Try This

It's sometimes hard to be in touch with our feelings. Try this for at least three days. As you live each of these three days, make a mental note of each feeling (not thought) that passes through you. At the end of each day, make a list of the feelings you had during the day. In your evening prayer take time to entrust these feelings and experiences to God, thanking God and asking God to help and comfort you.

___ Yes, I'll give it a try in the coming week.

Why Did My Friend Die?

Copy Two Side 1

How Would You Answer?

- How does God embrace those who take their own life?
- Why do people say that it was "God's plan" when someone dies?
- How do I get over the fear of my parents dying?
- How do I enroll for heaven?
- Do ghosts exist?

What Would You Do or Say?

You are in the hallway after the memorial service for a close friend or family member who has died. Someone approaches you to express their support and says, "It was God's will. When it's time for us to go, God takes us." How would you feel? What would you think? Say?

My Own Thoughts about Death

Write a response to each of the following:

1. One question I have about death is . . .

2. This is what I believe about life after death:

3. This is how I feel about my own death:

I have no fear	1	2	3	4	5	6	7	8	I'm afraid to die

because . . .

4. This is what I believe about heaven:

5. This is what I believe about hell:

6. This is what I believe about suicide:

7. This is what I believe about the importance of the death of Jesus on the cross:

8. This is what I believe about Easter and the resurrection of Jesus:

What Does the Bible Say?

Talk about 1 Thessalonians 4:13-14. How does our belief in Jesus Christ help us to understand the meaning of our own suffering and death?

Try This

Option 1: Take time to visit a funeral home near you. If possible, go with a friend or youth group. Ask the receptionist to give you information about preplanning a funeral. Is grief counseling offered by the funeral home?

Option 2: Interview your parent or guardian and ask that person about his or her thoughts on death and dying. Has that person made plans to prepare for his or her own death?

___ Yes, I'll give it a try in the coming week.

Why Do We Feel a Need to Cover Up Our Feelings? Copy Two Side 2

How Would You Answer?

- How do I stop feeling depressed?
- Why don't guys show their emotions?
- Why aren't people clear about their feelings?
- Is worrying a sin?
- Does love always hurt?
- Is it normal to be so lonely all the time?

What Would You Do or Say?

Though you are able to cover it up well, you have a constant feeling of sadness inside you. You're wondering if you might be depressed. Who can you talk to? What would you say? If you are depressed and need to go to a doctor, whom would you go to?

My Own Feelings

Write a response to each of the following: Here is a list of a variety of feelings. For each one, think of a time when you felt that way:

1. I felt happy when . . .
2. I felt relieved when . . .
3. I felt ashamed when . . .
4. I felt sad when . . .
5. I felt joyful when . . .
6. I felt confused when . . .
7. I felt depressed when . . .
8. I felt embarrassed when . . .
9. I felt loved when . . .

What Does the Bible Say?

Read John 14:1 and discuss how believing in Jesus can help troubled hearts. In addition, look at Romans 5:1-5 and talk about the advice Paul gives to those who are troubled and suffering.

Try This

It's sometimes hard to be in touch with our feelings. Try this for at least three days. As you live each of these three days, make a mental note of each feeling (not thought) that passes through you. At the end of each day, make a list of the feelings you had during the day. In your evening prayer take time to entrust these feelings and experiences to God, thanking God and asking God to help and comfort you.

___ Yes, I'll give it a try in the coming week.

Why Don't Guys Think Like Girls?

Copy One Side 1

How Would You Answer?

- How do you know the difference between true love and just a crush?
- Why don't guys think like girls?
- Why aren't girls and guys treated as equals?
- Is homosexuality hereditary?
- If men and women constantly drive each other crazy, why do we consistently put up with each other?

What Would You Do or Say?

You think you're in love with someone and would really like to spend more time with that person, but they show no interest in you. Is this normal? Who do you talk to about your feelings? What can you do about it?

My Own Thoughts about Girls or Guys

Write a response to each of the following:

1. Three words that describe most females (but not males):

2. Three words that describe most males (but not females):

3. Because males and females are different, it's a challenge for both males and females to . . .

4. Although there are differences, three ways we are all similar include:

5. One advantage of being female is . . .

6. One advantage of being male is . . .

7. I feel good that God made me who I am, because . . .

8. My prayer is: Dear God, help me in my own sexuality to feel good about . . .

What Does the Bible Say?

Read Jesus' teaching in Matthew 19:3-5. What does the Bible teach us about God's design for marriage? Why are there so many marriages that end in divorce?

Try This

Talk with a parent or guardian or another adult you trust about their experiences and challenges in understanding the opposite sex. You might want to ask them some of the questions above. Also, invite them to share their view of the marriage promise and why they believe so many marriages fail.

___ Yes, I'll give it a try in the coming week.

If We're Not Supposed to Have Premarital Sex, Then Why Do Hormones Kick in So Early?

Copy One Side 2

How Would You Answer?

- Is God pro-choice?
- Does everyone my age think about sex, or is it just me?
- Is masturbation a sin?
- Is sex for fun a sin?
- When is abstinence coming back?
- Why did Adam and Eve mess up the walkin'-around-naked idea?

What Would You Do or Say?

A very good friend of yours has just confided in you that she's pregnant, but she hasn't told anyone else, not even the guy. How do you respond? React? What do you say? What are some of her options? Where can she find help?

My Own Thoughts about Sex

Write a belief or thought you have about each of the following topics:

1. Sexual intimacy or intercourse before a committed relationship is established:

2. A lifelong, committed relationship with a spouse or partner:

3. Birth control before a committed relationship:

4. Sexual abstinence:

5. Masturbation:

6. Sexually transmitted diseases (including AIDS):

7. Homosexuality:

8. What do I do if I think I'm going too far sexually?

9. This is my commitment to God and to myself:

What Does the Bible Say?

Read Song of Solomon 8:6-7 and talk about how we honor God as sexual beings. What is God's understanding of human sexuality?

Try This

Choose to watch a TV program (either alone or with a friend or family member). Plan ahead of time to watch for sexual messages and values presented in the program or movie. Compare and talk about your own values and beliefs with those being presented by the media.

___ Yes, I'll give it a try in the coming week.

Why Don't Guys Think Like Girls?

How Would You Answer?

- How do you know the difference between true love and just a crush?
- Why don't guys think like girls?
- Why aren't girls and guys treated as equals?
- Is homosexuality hereditary?
- If men and women constantly drive each other crazy, why do we consistently put up with each other?

What Would You Do or Say?

You think you're in love with someone and would really like to spend more time with that person, but they show no interest in you. Is this normal? Who do you talk to about your feelings? What can you do about it?

My Own Thoughts about Girls or Guys

Write a response to each of the following:

1. Three words that describe most females (but not males):

2. Three words that describe most males (but not females):

3. Because males and females are different, it's a challenge for both males and females to . . .

4. Although there are differences, three ways we are all similar include:

5. One advantage of being female is . . .

6. One advantage of being male is . . .

7. I feel good that God made me who I am, because . . .

8. My prayer is: Dear God, help me in my own sexuality to feel good about . . .

What Does the Bible Say?

Read Jesus' teaching in Matthew 19:3-5. What does the Bible teach us about God's design for marriage? Why are there so many marriages that end in divorce?

Try This

Talk with a parent or guardian or another adult you trust about their experiences and challenges in understanding the opposite sex. You might want to ask them some of the questions above. Also, invite them to share their view of the marriage promise and why they believe so many marriages fail.

___ Yes, I'll give it a try in the coming week.

If We're Not Supposed to Have Premarital Sex, Then Why Do Hormones Kick in So Early?

Copy Two Side 2

How Would You Answer?

- Is God pro-choice?
- Does everyone my age think about sex, or is it just me?
- Is masturbation a sin?
- Is sex for fun a sin?
- When is abstinence coming back?
- Why did Adam and Eve mess up the walkin'-around-naked idea?

What Would You Do or Say?

A very good friend of yours has just confided in you that she's pregnant, but she hasn't told anyone else, not even the guy. How do you respond? React? What do you say? What are some of her options? Where can she find help?

My Own Thoughts about Sex

Write a belief or thought you have about each of the following topics:

1. Sexual intimacy or intercourse before a committed relationship is established:

2. A lifelong, committed relationship with a spouse or partner:

3. Birth control before a committed relationship:

4. Sexual abstinence:

5. Masturbation:

6. Sexually transmitted diseases (including AIDS):

7. Homosexuality:

8. What do I do if I think I'm going too far sexually?

9. This is my commitment to God and to myself:

What Does the Bible Say?

Read Song of Solomon 8:6-7 and talk about how we honor God as sexual beings. What is God's understanding of human sexuality?

Try This

Choose to watch a TV program (either alone or with a friend or family member). Plan ahead of time to watch for sexual messages and values presented in the program or movie. Compare and talk about your own values and beliefs with those being presented by the media.

___ Yes, I'll give it a try in the coming week.